THE BOOK OF COMFORT & JOY

Fear not, for I am with thee;
Be not dismayed,
for I am thy God.

I will strengthen thee;
Yea, I will help thee,
Yea, I will uphold thee with
the right hand
of my righteousness.

Isaiah 41:10

IDEALS PUBLISHING CORPORATION
NASHVILLE, TENNESSEE

ACKNOWLEDGMENTS

BE STRONG from *THOUGHTS FOR EVERYDAY LIVING* by Maltbie Davenport Babcock (New York: Charles Scribner's Sons, 1901); HOPE and OH, TO LIVE BEAUTIFULLY from *POEMS OF INSPIRATION AND COURAGE* by Grace Noll Crowell, Copyright 1936 by Harper & Row, Publishers, Inc., renewed © 1964 by Grace Noll Crowell. Reprinted by permission of Harper & Row, Publishers, Inc.; MOON COMPASSES and THE ROAD NOT TAKEN from *THE POETRY OF ROBERT FROST*, edited by Edward Connery Lathem. Copyright 1916, © 1969 by Holt, Rinehart and Winston, copyright 1936, 1944 by Robert Frost, © 1964 by Lesley Frost Ballantine. Reprinted by permission of Henry Holt and Company, Inc.; HOLD FAST YOUR DREAMS by Louise Driscoll from *THE HOME BOOK OF MODERN VERSE*, Burton Egbert Stevenson, editor. Copyright 1925 by Holt, Rinehart and Winston, copyright 1953 by Burton Egbert Stevenson. Reprinted by permission of Henry Holt and Company, Inc.; TO BUILD UP FAITH from *I'VE GOT TO TALK TO SOMEONE, GOD* by Marjorie Holmes, Copyright © 1969 by Marjorie Holmes Mighell. Used by permission of Doubleday, a division of Bantam, Doubleday, Dell Publishing Group, Inc.; MY HAND IN GOD'S by Florence Scripps Kellogg. Used by permission of the Unity School of Christianity, publisher of *DAILY WORD*; THE WAKING, Copyright 1953 by Theodore Roethke. From *THE COLLECTED POEMS OF THEODORE ROETHKE* by Theodore Roethke. Used by permission of Doubleday, a division of Bantam, Doubleday, Dell Publishing Group, Inc.; AFTERNOON ON A HILL by Edna St. Vincent Millay from *COLLECTED POEMS*, Harper & Row. Copyright 1917, 1945 by Edna St. Vincent Millay. Reprinted by permission; GOD'S WORLD by Edna St. Vincent Millay From *COLLECTED POEMS*, Harper & Row. Copyright 1913, 1941 by Edna St. Vincent Millay; A MORNING PRAYER from *COMPLETE POEMS OF ROBERT LOUIS STEVENSON* (New York: Charles Scribner's Sons, 1923); THE UNBROKEN STRING and HOPE IS LIKE THE SUN by Patience Strong. Used by permission of Rupert Crew Limited, London, ENGLAND; BARTER was reprinted by permission of Macmillan Publishing Company from *COLLECTED POEMS* by Sara Teasdale. Copyright 1917 by Macmillan Publishing Company, renewed 1945 by Mamie T. Wheless; A MILE WITH ME from *THE POEMS OF HENRY VAN DYKE*, Revised Edition (New York: Charles Scribner's Sons, 1920). Our sincere thanks to the following whose addresses we were unable to locate: Paul F. Barnett for THIS MOMENT; Betsey Buttles for I DO NOT ASK; the Estate of Mary Carolyn Davies for A PRAYER FOR EVERY DAY; Margaret Freer for PURPOSE; Elma V. Harnetiaux for HOPE IS A WORD TO LIVE BY; May Hayward Hunt for A MORNING WISH BY Walter Reid Hunt; Lura Bailey Jones for SUPPLICATION; Bernice C. Plautz for MY GUIDE; Edwin Roworth for LIFE'S RIPPLES; A.W. Spalding for HIGH ADVENTURE; Anna Vallance for BEAUTY IS ABROAD; the Estate of Nixon Waterman for FAR FROM THE MADDING CROWD from *A ROSE TO THE LIVING AND OTHER POEMS*, Copyright 1919, published by Chapple Publishing Company, Ltd., Boston; Esther Baldwin York for HOPE'S PROMISE.

Cover Photo
H. Armstrong Roberts

Cottongrass
Mt. McKinley, Alaska
Jeff Gnass

CONTENTS

Comfort from Faith

Sunlight through Pine Trees
H. Armstrong Roberts

*Faith is the substance of things hoped for,
the evidence of things unseen.*

Hebrews 11:1

High Adventure

As I have seen a child,
Round-eyed and innocent,
Leaving his treasured playthings piled
Where new adventure overtook,
Climb up a little staired ascent,
Holding in fear his parent's hand,
And, trepidant with fresh alarms
Yet gathering courage from each trustful look,
With utter confidence in a last command,
Fling himself laughing into his father's arms—

So I, another child,
Holding my Father's hand,
Now from my busy arts beguiled
By what He promises beyond,
Forgetting all that I have planned,
And pressing on with faith's sure sight
O'er rock and ridge, through mists and storms,
With confidence that swallows up despond,
From the last crag of life's most glorious height
Cast me exultant into my Father's arms.

A.W. Spalding

Antelope Valley, California
Alpha Photo Inc.

I Have Faith

I have faith in the new day that's coming,
    in the things that I know I shall do;

I have faith that there'll be something lovely for me,
    and I've faith in myself, have you?

I believe that our God will watch over,
    and I know that he'll always take care;

And if things go wrong, we shall still have a song
    and a happiness always to share.

That's why I have faith in tomorrow,
    though today might be lonely and blue;

My best I shall give, in each new day I live,
    and my own faith shall carry me through.

Garnett Ann Schultz

My Guide

"Walk close to me, my child," he said,
    And on the way, he gently led;
"I know the way, it's very steep,
    But do not fear, for I can keep
Your way secure; just trust me more."
    And so I walk the road of life—
My hand in his; no fear, no strife;
    He keeps my heart rejoicing
In every testing; none is too great.
    Because of him my heart is singing;
He leads the way through every day.
    I'm in this world for just a while;
I'll trust him when I go through trials.
    And often as I kneel and pray
I ask him for the words to say
    So others will be drawn to him
By what they see of him in me.
    I ask him to show me the need
Of each one for whom I should pray,
    The ones I meet from day to day.
He guides my thoughts, my lips, my feet,
    And teaches me just how to speak—
Sometimes, with joy, sometimes a warning,
    Always with love to meet their longing.
I never fear with him to guide,
    On the stony road I do not fall;
I have my friend close by my side;
    I cling to him when I feel weak;
He always hears me when I call.
    He never fails! His strength is mine;
    I walk with him in joy sublime!

Bernice C. Plautz

All Times Are God's Season

We ask our daily bread, and God never says, You should have come yesterday. He never says, You must come again tomorrow. But "today if you will hear His voice," today He will hear you.

If some king of the earth has so large an extent of dominion in north and south as that he hath winter and summer together in his dominions, so large an extent of east and west as that he hath day and night together in his dominions, much more hath God mercy and judgment together.

He brought light out of darkness, not out of a lesser light. He can bring thy summer out of winter though thou have no spring.

Though in the ways of fortune, or misunderstanding, or conscience, thou have been benighted till now, wintered and frozen, clouded and eclipsed, damp and benumbed, smothered and stupefied till now, now God comes to thee, not as in dawning of the day, not as in the bud of the spring, but as the sun at noon, to banish all shadows; as the sheaves in harvest, to fill all penuries. All occasions invite His mercies, and all times are His season.

God made sun and moon to distinguish seasons, and day and night; and we cannot have the fruits of the earth but in their seasons. But God hath made no decrees to distinguish the seasons of His mercies. In Paradise the fruits were ripe the first minute, and in Heaven it is always autumn; His mercies are ever in their maturity.

John Donne

The Voice of Faith

I have seen a curious child, who dwelt upon a tract
Of inland ground, applying to his ear
The convolutions of a smooth-lipped shell;
To which, in silence hushed, his very soul
Listened intensely; for from within were heard
Murmurings, whereby the monitor expressed
Mysterious union with its native sea.
Even such a shell the universe itself
Is to the ear of faith; and there are times,
I doubt not, when to you it doth impart
Authentic tidings of invisible things,
Of ebb and flow, and ever-enduring power,
And central peace, subsisting at the heart
Of endless agitation.

William Wordsworth

To Build up Faith

God, please help me to build up my faith.
Let me understand that faith is not a blind acceptance,
    But a certain and reasonable knowledge.
Not a gift bestowed upon favored people,
    But a powerful conviction achieved through serious effort.

God, guide me to people who can encourage me in my faith.
    (Thank you for such people.)
Lead me to books that will enlighten and enhance my faith.
    (Thank you for such books.)
Show me works both human and divine that prove
    That you do exist and love us.
Open my eyes to your many wonders.

Free my cluttered and limited mind from its confusion.
Release it, refresh it, widen it so that into it may flow an
    Appreciation of your vast, shining, limitless intelligence.
    (Thank you for that clearing and that comprehension now.)

Help me to practice my faith, for only through practice
    Can it grow in me.
Oh, God, remind me to reach you and understand you,
    And renew my faith through prayer.

Marjorie Holmes

What Is the Grass?

A child said, What is the grass?
Fetching it to me with full hands,
How could I answer the child?
I do not know what it is any more than he.

I guess it must be the flag of my disposition,
Out of hopeful green stuff woven.

Or I guess it is the handkerchief of the Lord,
A scented gift and remembrancer designedly dropt,
Bearing the owner's name someway in the corners,
That we may see and remark, and say Whose?

Walt Whitman

Hay Bales
Door County, Wisconsin
Laatsch-Hupp Photographers

Joy of Beauty

Red Barn with
Cosmos and Zinnias
Lovel, Vermont
Gay Bumgarner

Though we travel the world over to find the beautiful, we must carry it with us or we find it not.

Ralph Waldo Emerson   *Joy of Beauty* 21

Once More Tall

When I behold the heavens, Lord,
   The sun and moon and stars,
And think upon the worlds that lie
   Beyond the planet Mars,

I shrink into my smallest self,
   Even smaller than a mote,
And wonder God should take of me
   The very slightest note.

Then I see the sparrows in the wind
   And know God marks their fall;
My soul swells up with God's great love,
   And I am once more tall.

Minnie Klemme

God's World

O world, I cannot hold thee close enough!
Thy winds, thy wide grey skies!
Thy mists, that roll and rise!
Thy woods, this autumn day, that ache and sag
And all but cry with colour! That gaunt crag
To crush! To lift the lean of the black bluff!
World, World, I cannot get thee close enough!

Long have I known a glory in it all,
But never knew I this:
Here such a passion is
As stretcheth me apart,—Lord, I do fear
Thou'st made the world too beautiful this year;
My soul is all but out of me,—let fall
No burning leaf; prithee, let no bird call.

Edna St. Vincent Millay

Oh, to Live Beautifully

Oh, to live beautifully
For my brief hour
As does a wayside flower,
Unperturbed by the strange brevity
Of time allotted me;
Undisturbed by the overshadowing shine
Of tree and climbing vine;
Bravely stemming the wind and the beating rain,
Bowing and lifting again;
Within me some strong inner force as bright
As a poppy filled with light;
My feet firm-rooted in the earth's good sod,
My face turned toward God,
Yielding some fragrance down the paths I know
A little while . . . then go
As a flower goes, its petals seeking the ground
Without a cry or sound,
But leaving behind some gold seed lightly thinned
To blow upon the wind.

Grace Noll Crowell

Pied Beauty

Glory be to God
    for dappled things—
For skies of couple-colour
    as a brinded cow;

For rose-moles all in stipple
    upon trout that swim;
Fresh-firecoal chestnut-falls;
    finches' wings;

Landscape plotted and pierced—
    fold, fallow, and plough;
And all trades, their gear
    and tackle and trim.

All things counter,
    original, spare, strange;
Whatever is fickle, freckled
    (who knows how?)
With swift, slow; sweet, sour;
    adazzle, dim;
He fathers-forth whose beauty
    is past change:
Praise him.

Gerard Manley Hopkins

Endymion

A thing of beauty is a joy forever:
Its loveliness increases; it will never
Pass into nothingness; but still will keep
A bower quiet for us, and a sleep
Full of sweet dreams, and health, and quiet breathing.
Therefore, on every morrow, are we wreathing
A flowery band to bind us to the earth,
Spite of despondence, of the inhuman dearth
Of noble natures, of the gloomy days.
Of all the unhealthy and o'er-darkened ways
Made for our searching: yes, in spite of all,
Some shape of beauty moves away the pall
From our dark spirits. Such the sun, the moon,
Trees old and young, sprouting a shady boon
For simple sheep; and such are daffodils
With the green world they live in; and clear rills
That for themselves a cooling covert make
'Gainst the hot season; the mid-forest brake,
Rich with a sprinkling of fair musk-rose blooms:
And such too is the grandeur of the dooms
We have imagined for the mighty dead;
All lovely tales that we have heard or read:
An endless fountain of immortal drink,
Pouring unto us from the heaven's brink.
Nor do we merely feel these essences
For one short hour; no, even as the trees
That whisper round a temple become soon
Dear as the temple's self, so does the moon,
The passion posey, glories infinite,
Haunt us till they become a cheering light
Unto our souls, and bound to us so fast,
That, whether there be shine, or gloom o'ercast,
They always must be with us, or we die.

John Keats

Waterlilies
H. Armstrong Roberts

Beauty Is Abroad

Beauty is abroad in the land today,
In the wild flowers blooming along the way,
In the changing green in the light on the trees.
Its voice is heard in the whispering breeze,
In the rippling stream as it glides along,
In the happy notes of the bluebird's song.
It climbs a hill, glides over the ridge
And spans a stream at a rustic bridge.
Oh, beauty is abroad in the land today
In many guises along the way.

Beauty is abroad in the land today,
It smiles and beckons along the way.
It dances gaily in a field of flowers
And plays hide and seek in leafy bowers.
It's flung like a robe over pastures green,
It rides on a cloud or a pale moonbeam.
It's hiding deep in the heart of a rose,
It lurks in the field where the violet grows.
Oh beauty is abroad in the land today. . .
And it's forever there beside the way.

Anna Vallance

The Rhodora

In May, when sea-winds pierced our solitudes,
I found the fresh Rhodora in the woods,
Spreading its leafless blooms in a damp nook,
To please the desert and the sluggish brook.

The purple petals, fallen in the pool,
Made the black water with their beauty gay;
Here might the redbird come his plumes to cool,
And court the flower that cheapens his array.

Rhodora! If the sages ask thee why
This charm is wasted on the earth and sky,
Tell them, dear, that if eyes were made for seeing,
Then Beauty is its own excuse for being.

Why thou wert there, O rival of the rose!
I never thought to ask, I never knew:
But, in my simple ignorance, suppose
The self-same Power that brought me there brought you.

Ralph Waldo Emerson

Comfort through Love

Road through Fall Trees
New York
Comstock

Love comforteth like sunshine after rain.

William Shakespeare

A Mile with Me

O who will walk a mile with me
Along life's merry way?
A comrade blithe and full of glee,
Who dares to laugh out loud and free,
And let his frolic fancy play,
Like a happy child, through the flowers gay
That fill the field and fringe the way
Where he walks a mile with me.

And who will walk a mile with me
Along life's weary way?
A friend whose heart has eyes to see
The stars shine out o'er the darkening lea,
And the quiet rest at the end o' the day,
A friend who knows, and dares to say,
The brave, sweet words that cheer the way
Where he walks a mile with me.

With such a comrade, such a friend,
I fain would walk till journey's end,
Through summer sunshine, winter rain,
And then?—Farewell, we shall meet again!

Henry van Dyke

Love the World

There is so much I have not been,
So much I have not seen.
I have not thought and have not done
Or felt enough—the early sun,
Rain and the seasonal delight
Of flocks of ducks and geese in flight,
The mysteries of late-at-night.

I still need time to read a book,
Write poems, paint a picture, look
At scenes and faces dear to me.
There is something more to be
Of value—something I should find
Within myself—as peace of mind,
Patience, grace, and being kind.

I shall take and I shall give
While yet, there is so much to live
For—rainbows, stars that gleam,
The fields, the hills, the hope, the dream,
The truth that one must seek. I'll stay
Here—treasure every day
And love the world in my own way!

Helen Harrington

Canadian Geese in Flight
Appel

Barter

Life has loveliness to sell,
All beautiful and splendid things,
Blue waves whitened on a cliff,
Soaring fire that sways and sings,
And children's faces looking up
Holding wonder like a cup.

Life has loveliness to sell,
Music like a curve of gold,
Scent of pine trees in the rain,
Eyes that love you, arms that hold,
And for your spirit's still delight,
Holy thoughts that star the night.

Spend all you have for loveliness,
Buy it and never count the cost;
For one white singing hour of peace
Count many a year of strife well lost,
And for a breath of ecstasy
Give all you have been or could be.

Sara Teasdale

Answer to a Child's Question

Do you ask what the birds say?
The sparrow, the dove,
The linnet and thrush say,
"I love and I love!"
In the winter they're silent—
The wind is so strong;
What it says, I don't know,
But it sings a loud song.
But green leaves, and blossoms,
And sunny warm weather,
And singing, and loving—
All come back together.
But the lark is so brimful
Of gladness and love,
The green fields below him
The blue sky above,
That he sings, and he sings;
And for ever sings he—
"I love my Love,
And my Love loves me!"

Samuel Taylor Coleridge

Perfect Love

Perfect love has this advantage in it,
That it leaves the possessor of it
Nothing further to desire.
There is one object (at least)
In which the soul finds absolute content,
For which it seeks to live,
Or dares to die.
The heart has, as it were,
Filled up the moulds of the imagination.
The truth of passion keeps pace with
And outvies the extravagance of mere language.
There are no words so fine,
No flattery so soft,
That there is not a sentiment beyond them,
That it is impossible to express,
At the bottom of the heart where true love is.
What idle sounds the common phrases,
Adorable creature, angel, divinity, are!
What a proud reflection it is to have
A feeling answering to all these,
Rooted in the breast, unalterable, unutterable,
To which all other feelings are light and vain!
Perfect love reposes on the object of its choice,
Like the halcyon on the wave;
And the air of heaven is around it.

William Hazlitt

A Day

What does it take to make a day?
A lot of love along the way:
It takes a morning and a noon,
A father's voice, a mother's croon;
It takes some task to challenge all
The powers that a man may call
His own: the powers of mind and limb;
A whispered word of love; a hymn
Of hope—a comrade's cheer—
A baby's laughter and a tear;
It takes a dream, a hope, a cry
Of need from some soul passing by;
A sense of brotherhood and love;
A purpose sent from God above;
It takes a sunset in the sky,
The stars of night, the winds that sigh;
It takes a breath of scented air
A mother's kiss, a baby's prayer.
That is what it takes to make a day;
A lot of love along the way.

William L. Stidger

Love

Love is the only bow on life's dark cloud.
It is the Morning and the Evening Star.
It shines upon the cradle of the babe,
    and sheds its radiance
Upon the quiet tomb.

It is the mother of Art, inspirer of Poet,
    patriot and philosopher.
It is the air and light of every heart,
    builder of every home,
Kindler of every fire on every hearth.
It was the first to dream of immortality.
It fills the world with melody,
    for Music is the voice of Love.

Love is the magician, the enchanter,
    that changes worthless things to joy,
And makes right royal kings
    and queens of common clay.
It is the perfume of the wondrous flower—
    the heart—and without that sacred passion,
    that divine swoon, we are less than beasts;
But with it, earth is heaven and we are gods.

Robert Ingersoll

Joy in Imagination

String Lake
Grand Teton National Park, Wyoming
H. Armstrong Roberts

They can because they think they can

Virgil

Day!

Faster and more fast,
O'er night's brim, day boils at last;
Boils, pure gold, o'er the cloud-cap's brim
Where spurting and suppressed it lay,
For not a froth-flake touched the rim
Of yonder gap in the solid gray
Of the eastern cloud, an hour away;
But forth one wavelet, then another, curled,
Till the whole sunrise, not to be suppressed,
Rose, reddened, and its seething breast
Flickered in bounds, grew gold,
Then overflowed the world.

Robert Browning

Supplication

Give me a heart attuned to simple glories—
Leaf-dappled trails beneath my eager feet;

Bright little streams, bordered by slender willows;
The quiet hills, the meadows summer sweet.

Let me store deep in memory's chest the treasures
Of golden dawn and sunset, autumn trees;

Lapis lazuli skies and silver moonlight.
Perhaps sometimes I may have need of these.

And let me remember stars against that time
That I may feel the need to touch a star.

And tulips for the day I may not go
To find God in a spot where tulips are.

Lura Bailey Jones

The Waking

I strolled across an open field;
The sun was out; Heat was happy.

This way! This way!
The wren's throat shimmered,
Either to other the blossoms sang.

The stones sang, the little ones did,
And flowers jumped like small goats.

A ragged fringe of daisies waved;
I wasn't alone in a grove of apples.

Far in the wood a nestling sighed;
The dew loosened its morning smells.

I came where the river ran over stones;
My ears knew an early joy.

And all the waters of all the streams
Sang in my veins that summer day.

Theodore Roethke

Canadian Snow Geese
Cap Tourmente, Quebec
Canada
Reflexion

Moon Compasses

I stole forth dimly in the dripping pause
Between two downpours to see what there was.
And a masked moon had spread down compass rays
To a cone mountain in the midnight haze,
As if the final estimate were hers;
And as it measured in her calipers,
The mountain stood exalted in its place.
So love will take between the hands a face. . .

Robert Frost

Hold Fast Your Dreams

Hold fast your dreams!
Within your heart keep one still, secret spot
Where dreams may go, and, sheltered so,
May thrive and grow where doubt and fear are not.
O keep a place apart, within your heart,
For little dreams to go!

Think still of lovely things that are not true.
Let wish and magic work at will in you.
Be sometimes blind to sorrow. Make believe!
Forget the calm that lies in disillusioned eyes.
Though we all know that we must die,
Yet you and I may walk like gods and be
Even now at home in immortality.
We see so many ugly things—
Deceits and wrongs and quarrelings;
We know, alas! we know how quickly fade
The color in the west, the bloom upon the flower,
The bloom upon the breast and youth's blind hour.
Yet keep within your heart a place apart
Where little dreams may go, may thrive and grow.
Hold fast—hold fast your dreams!

Louise Driscoll

I Wandered Lonely as a Cloud

I wandered lonely as a cloud
    that floats on high o'er vales and hills,
When all at once I saw a crowd,
    a host of golden daffodils
Beside the lake, beneath the trees,
    fluttering and dancing in the breeze.

Continuous as the stars that shine
    and twinkle on the Milky Way,
They stretched in never-ending line
    along the margin of a bay:
Ten thousand saw I, at a glance,
    tossing their heads in sprightly dance.

The waves beside them danced, but they
    outdid the sparkling waves in glee;
A poet could not but be gay
    in such a jocund company;
I gazed—and gazed—but little thought
    what wealth the show to me had brought.

For oft, when on my couch I lie,
    in vacant or in pensive mood,
They flash upon that inward eye
    which is the bliss of solitude;
And then my heart with pleasure fills
    and dances with the daffodils.

William Wordsworth

Comfort in Hope

Sapphire Beach, Virgin Islands
H. Armstrong Roberts

Hope springs eternal in the human breast.

Alexander Pope

Hope Is Like the Sun

Hope is like the sun
   Upon the threshold of the heart.
A glow lights up the inner room.
   The shadows fall apart,
And rising to unlatch the door
   We cast all fear away
As we venture out into
   The brightness of the day.

Hope is like a ray of sunlight
   Falling on gray stone.
The heart is warmed.
   We're tempted out
To take the road alone,
   Out towards a broad horizon
Where the sky is gold
   With promise of the love of God
And blessings manifold.

Patience Strong

My Hand in God's

Each morning when I wake I say,
"I place my hand in God's today."
I know He'll walk close by my side,
My every wandering step to guide.

He leads me with the tenderest care
When paths are dark and I despair.
No need for me to understand,
If I but hold fast to His hand.

My hand in His! No surer way
To walk in safety through each day.
By His great bounty I am fed,
Warmed by His love, and comforted.

When at day's end I seek my rest
And realize how much I'm blessed,
My thanks pour out to Him; and then
I place my hand in God's again.

Florence Scripps Kellogg

Yuccas at Sunset
Near Oracle, Arizona
Josef Muench

Hope Is a Word to Live By

Hope is a word to live by.
Hope is something within us that makes
    us strive and reach for something higher.
There may be failure, but there is always hope
    to start again, with hope directing our way.

Hope longs for a desired goal.
Hope keeps us with a song in our hearts.
Hope is a booster for the discouraged.
Hope is a stepping stone to the depressed and
    needy; it renews their will to find a brighter day.

Hope is confidence and expectation.
Hope is a guide to good cheer and happiness.
Hope is a comfort when fear assails us.
Hope brings light into darkness.
Hope is truly a word to live by.

Elma V. Harnetiaux

Hope

This would I hold more precious than fine gold,
This would I keep although all else be lost:
Hope in my heart, that precious, priceless thing,
      hope at any cost.

And God, if its fine luster should be dimmed,
If seemingly through grief it may be spent,
Help me to wait without too much despair —
      too great astonishment.

Let me be patient when my spirit lacks
Its high exuberance, its shining wealth;
Hope is a matter often, God, I know,
      of strength . . . of health.

Help me to wait until the strength returns;
Help me to climb each difficult high slope;
Always within my heart some golden gleam—
      some quenchless spark of hope.

Grace Noll Crowell

The Unbroken String

Love and friendship, joy and sorrow,
These are the strings on which we play.
These are the notes that go to make
The varied music of the day.

With the passing of the years
The strings of life get frayed and thin—
And youth's high tones are touched
With sadness, like a muted violin.

But there is one undying thing,
One golden string that does not break:
The string of Hope—

We play upon it, and it never fails to wake
An echo in the weary spirit.
One sweet note fresh faith can bring.

For Hope is the music of the soul
Played on the heart's unbroken string.

Patience Strong

Hope

Hope
Is a robin singing
On a rainy day;

He knows
The sun will shine again
Though skies may now be gray.

Like the robin
Let us be,
Meet trouble
With a smile;
And the sun
Will shine for us
In just a little while.

Beverly J. Anderson

One Day at a Time

Finish every day
And be done with it.
You have done what you could.

Some blunders and absurdities
No doubt crept in;
Forget them as soon as you can.

Tomorrow is a new day;
Begin it well and serenely
And with too high a spirit
To be cumbered with your old nonsense.

This day is all that is good and fair.
It is too dear,
With its hopes and invitations,
To waste a moment on the yesterdays.

Ralph Waldo Emerson

Hope's Promise

Hope is
A looking forward to something
With an earnest belief.

Often it means
An expectancy of light
When one is still in darkness.

I like to think of it
As the promise of dawn
To follow the night shadows.

Life takes new strength
And meaning
Where there is hope.

Let us keep this promise
In our hearts.

Esther Baldwin York

Joy in Prayer

Country Church
Near Waupaca, Wisconsin
Ken Dequaine

Prayer is the wing wherewith the soul flies to heaven.

Saint Ambrose

The Lord Is My Shepherd

The Lord is my shepherd; I shall not want.
He maketh me to lie down in green pastures;
He leadeth me beside the still waters.

He restoreth my soul; He leadeth me in the
Paths of righteousness for His name's sake.
Yea, though I walk through the valley of the
Shadow of death, I will fear no evil, for Thou
Art with me; Thy rod and Thy staff they comfort me.

Thou preparest a table before me in the presence of
Mine enemies; Thou annointest my head with oil;
My cup runneth over.

Surely goodness and mercy shall follow me all the days of
My life: and I will dwell in the house of the Lord forever.

Psalm 23

In an Old Church

The faded frescoes do not touch my heart
Nor ancient altarpiece nor rood nor choir,
With reverence translated into art.
Each soaring column, vaulted arch and spire
Awakens admiration, but I feel
Less moved by them than lighted candles' glow
And stone worn deeply where the people kneel
As ceaseless generations come and go.

Nine hundred years of prayer encircle me,
With deepest aspirations, joy and grief.
The song of faith resounds exultantly
To tell the age-old triumph of belief.
Encompassed by an unseen host today,
My pilgrim soul now pauses here to pray.

Gail Brook Burket

Purpose

Dear Lord, may others find in me
A pool of cool tranquility;
A quiet resting place to find
New strength of heart and peace of mind.

May all who stop within my gate
Find solace here; exchange the hate
For love that ever-widening dwells
Outside the circle of themselves.

And may I have the listening ear
That helps dispel all doubt and fear.
In days of dark uncertainty,
Lord, place an inner light in me.

Lord, should my inner light be low,
Help Thy unfailing grace to grow,
That all who come to me with care
May see Thy love reflected there.

Margaret Freer

A Morning Prayer

The day returns
And brings us the petty round
Of irritating concerns and duties.

Help us to play the man,
Help us to perform them
With laughter and kind faces,
Let cheerfulness abound with industry.

Give us to go blithely
On our business all this day,
Bring us to our resting beds
Weary and content and undishonored,
And grant us in the end
The gift of sleep.

Robert Louis Stevenson

A Prayer for Every Day

Make me too brave to lie or be unkind,
Make me too understanding, too, to mind
The little hurts companions give, and friends,
The careless hurts that no one quite intends.
Make me too thoughtful to hurt others so.
Help me to know
The inmost hearts of those for whom I care,
Their secret wishes, all the loads they bear,
That I might add my courage to their own.

May I make lonely folks feel less alone,
And happy ones a little happier yet.
May I forget
What ought to be forgotten; and recall
Unfailing, all
That ought to be recalled, each kindly thing,
Forgetting what might sting.
To all upon my way,
Day after day,
Let me be joy, be hope—Let my life sing!

Mary Carolyn Davies

How Manifold
Are Thy Works

Who laid the foundations of the earth,
   That it should not be removed for ever.

He sendeth the spring into the valleys,
   Which run among the hills.
He watereth the hills from his chambers:
   The earth is satisfied with the fruit of thy works.

He appointed the moon for seasons:
   The sun knoweth his going down.
Thou makest darkness, and it is night,
   Wherein all beasts of the forest do creep forth.

O Lord, how manifold are thy works!
   In wisdom hast thou made them all;
The earth is full of thy riches.

The sun ariseth, they gather themselves together,
   And lay them down in their dens.
The glory of the Lord shall endure forever:
   The Lord shall rejoice in his works.

I will sing unto the lord as long as I live:
I will sing praise to my God while I have my being,

from Psalm 104

Comfort from Peace

West Bay, Osterville,
Cape Cod, Massachusetts
Dick Smith

Blessed are the peacemakers:
for they shall be called the children of God.

Matthew 5:9

The Road Not Taken

Two roads diverged in a yellow wood,
And sorry I could not travel both
And be one traveler, long I stood
And looked down one as far as I could
To where it bent in the undergrowth;

Then took the other, as just as fair,
And having perhaps the better claim,
Because it was grassy and wanted wear;
Though as for that, the passing there
Had worn them really about the same,

And both that morning equally lay
In leaves no step had trodden black.
Oh, I kept the first for another day!
Yet knowing how way leads on to way,
I doubted if I should ever come back.

I shall be telling this with a sigh
Somewhere ages and ages hence:
Two roads diverged in a wood, and I
I took the one less traveled by,
And that has made all the difference.

Robert Frost

Give Me
a Humble Spirit, Lord

Give me a humble spirit, Lord,
Where wisdom will take root
And help me then to cultivate
Each tender, budding shoot;

Endow me with a thirst for truth,
Deny me self-content,
And make me useful in this world
Until my life is spent.

Give me a faith that's strong and sure
Above all temporal things,
Give me a sense of humor to
Offset life's tiresome stings.

And finally, Lord, make me sincere
In all I do and say
That I may build an inner fort
Which nothing can dismay.

Viney Wilder Endicott

Pinkham Notch, New Hampshire
Winter stream
Fred Sieb

Contentment

Contentment is that bit of golden light
That touches hearts and makes them clearly shine,
That brings a new depth into human sight
And makes just simple things seem rich and fine.

It may be part of evening fireside talks
Or just a smile across a table length,
It may surround a woods on autumn walks
Or brighten faith with new-discovered strength.

Contentment is that ray that warms the soul
And gives new courage where it may be found;
It follows hearts across the farthest knoll,
And lucky is that heart where it abounds.

Contentment is a light that all may see
Whose source is found in great eternity.

Maxine McCray Miller

Porch Memories
Camerique

I Do Not Ask

I do not ask that every dawn be radiant,
Or constant sunshine fall across my way.
But only that despite the clouds o'erspreading
My faith may make today a sun-filled day.

I do not ask great joy at every turning,
Upon the path my feet have learned to tread,
But only that I recognize the gladness
That love today about my steps has spread.

I do not ask that sometime I may enter some far-off
Heaven whose countless ages roll.
But only that in finding truth illuminated
I gain a Heaven today within my soul.

Betsey Buttles

Peace

Peace is looking at a child
With eyelids closed in sleep
And knowing that the love of God
Is constant, true, and deep.

Peace is gazing into depths
Of water, cool and clear,
And knowing fast within your heart
That God is ever near.

Peace is hearing birds that sing
In harmony of voice,
And knowing that you, too, can live
With God's own way your choice.

Peace is living day by day
With His own company,
So you will have within your soul
Divine tranquility.

Mildred Spires Jacobs

Far from
the Madding Crowd

It seems to me I'd like to go
Where bells don't ring, nor whistles blow,
Nor clocks don't strike, nor gongs sound,
And I'd have stillness all around.

Not real stillness, but just the trees
Low whispering, or the hum of bees,
Or brooks faint babbling over stones,
In strangely, softly tangled tones.

Or maybe a cricket or a katydid,
Or the songs of birds in the hedges hid,
Or just some such sweet sound as these,
To fill a tired heart with ease.

If 'tweren't for sight and sound and smell,
I'd like the city pretty well,
But when it comes to getting rest,
I like the country lots the best.

Sometimes it seems to me I must
Just quit the city's din and dust,
And get out where the sky is blue,
And say, now, how does it seem to you?

Nixon Waterman

Makest Me Dwell in Safety

Hear me when I call,
    O God of my righteousness:
Thou hast enlarged me
    when I was in distress:
Have mercy upon me
    and hear my prayer.

There be many that say,
    Who will show us any good?
Lord, lift thou up the light
    of thy countenance upon us.

Thou hast put gladness
    in my heart.
I will both lay me down
    in peace, and sleep:
For thou, Lord, only makest
    me dwell in safety.

from Psalm 4

Thompson Falls, Montana
Bob Firth

Joy in Wisdom

How much better is it to get wisdom than gold!

Proverbs 16:16

There Was a Child Went Forth

There was a child went forth every day;
And the first object he looked upon, the object he became;
And that object became part of him for the day,
   Or a certain part of the day, or for many years,
   Or stretching cycles of years:

The early lilacs became part of this child;
And the apple-trees covered with blossoms, and the fruit
   Afterward, and wood-berries, and the commonest weeds by the road;

The blow, the quick loud word, the tight bargain, the crafty lure,
The family usages, the language, the company, the furniture—
   The yearning and swelling heart;
The doubts of day-time and the doubts of night-time—
   The curious whether and how,
Whether that which appears so is so, or is it all flashes and specks?
Men and women crowding fast in the streets—
   If they are not flashes and specks, what are they?

These became part of that child who went forth every day,
And who now goes, and will always go forth every day.

Walt Whitman

Wisdom

Happy is the man that findeth wisdom,
And the man that getteth understanding.
For the merchandise of it is better
Than the merchandise of silver,
And the gain thereof than fine gold.

She is more precious than rubies:
And all things thou canst desire are not
To be compared unto her.

Length of days is in her right hand;
And in her left hand riches and honor.
Her ways are ways of pleasantness,
And all her paths are peace.

The Lord by wisdom hath founded the earth;
By understanding hath he established the heavens.
By his knowledge the depths are broken up,
And the clouds drop down the dew.
My son, let not them depart from thine eyes:
Keep sound wisdom and discretion.

from Proverbs 3

Greatness

A man is as great
   as the dreams he dreams,
As great as the love he bears,
   as great as the values he redeems,
As the happiness he shares.

A man is as great
   as the thoughts he thinks,
As the worth he has attained,
   as the fountains at which his spirit drinks,
As the insight he has gained.

A man is as great
   as the truth he speaks,
As great as the help he gives,
   as great as the destiny he seeks,
As great as the life he lives.

Author Unknown

White bark Pine
Sawtooth Lake
Sawtooth National Forest, Idaho
Jeff Gnass

For This Is Wisdom

For this is wisdom;
To love, to live,
To take what fate,
Or the gods, may give,
To ask no question,
To make no prayer,
To kiss the lips
And caress the hair,
Speed passion's ebb
As you greet its flow,
To have, to hold,
And—in time—let go!

Laurence Hope

Let Every Dawn

Let every dawn
   Of morning
Be to you as the beginning
   Of life,
And every setting sun
   Be to you
   As its close;

Then let every one
   Of these short lives
Leave its sure record
   Of some kindly thing
   Done for others,
Some goodly strength
   Or knowledge
   Gained for yourself.

John Ruskin

To Know Joy

The joy of life is living it
    and doing things of worth,
In making bright and fruitful
    all the barren spots on earth.

In facing odds and mastering them
    and rising from defeat,
And making true what once was false,
    and what was bitter, sweet.

For only he knows perfect joy
    whose little bit of soil
Is richer ground than what it was
    when he began to toil.

Author Unknown

Dream Pedlary

If there were dreams to sell,
What would you buy?

Some cost a passing bell;
Some a light sigh,

That shakes from Life's fresh crown
Only a rose-leaf down.

If there were dreams to sell,
Merry and sad to tell,

And the crier rang the bell,
What would you buy?

A cottage lone and still,
With bowers nigh,

Shadowy, my woes to still,
Until I die.

Such pearl from Life's fresh crown
Fain would I shake me down.

Were dreams to have at will,
This would best heal my ill,
This would I buy.

Thomas L. Beddoes

Comfort of Kindness

Early Autum
Iov
H. Armstrong Robe

*Do all the good you can, by all
the means you can.*

John Wesley

Comfort

Oh, the comfort—
The inexpressible comfort
Of feeling safe with a person,
Having neither to weigh thoughts,
Nor measure words—
But pouring them
All right out—
Just as they are—
Chaff and grain together—
Certain that a faithful hand
Will take and sift them—
Keep what is worth keeping—
And with the breath of kindness
Blow the rest away.

Dinah Maria Mulock Craik

A Morning Wish

The sun is just rising on the morning of another day. What can I wish that this day may bring me? Nothing that shall make the world or others poorer, nothing at the expense of other men, but just those few things which in their coming do not stop with me but touch me, rather, as they pass and gather strength.

A few friends who understand me, and yet remain my friends. . .
A mind unafraid to travel, even though the trail be not blazed.

A sight of the eternal hills and the unresting sea and of something beautiful which the hand of man has made. A sense of humor and the power to laugh. A little leisure with nothing to do.

A few moments of quiet, silent meditation. The sense of the presence of God. And the patience to wait for the coming of these things, with the wisdom to know them when they come, and the wit not to change this morning wish of mine.

Walter Reid Hunt

Life's Ripples

A tiny pebble idly tossed
Into the placid stream,
With gentle splash it sinks from sight
And not again is seen.
But outward from that central spot
The circling ripples tend,
Who knows on what far distant shore
The spreading impulse ends?

And so it is with life itself;
A word we say—a deed we do
May take a moment of our time
And then be lost to view,
But ever onward it will go
And never lost shall be,
Until its widening mission done,
It joins infinity.

Edwin Roworth

Bridge at Warner, New Hampshire
Fred Sieb

Out in the Fields with God

The little cares that fretted me,
    I lost them yesterday
Among the fields above the sea,
    among the winds that play,
Among the lowing of the herds,
    the rustling of the trees,
Among the singing of the birds,
    the humming of the bees.

The fears of what may come to pass,
    I cast them all away
Among the clover-scented grass,
    among the new-mown hay,
Among the rustling of the corn,
    where drowsy poppies nod,
Where ill thoughts die and good are born,
    out in the fields with God.

Author Unknown

Reward of Service

The sweetest lives are those to duty wed,
Whose deeds both great and small
Are close-knit strands of an unbroken thread,
Where love ennobles all.
The world may sound no trumpets, ring no bells,
The Book of Life the slurring record tells.

Thy love shall chant its own beatitudes,
After its own like working. A child's kiss
Set on thy singing lips shall make thee rich;
A sick man helped by thee shall make thee strong;
Thou shalt be served thyself by every sense
Of service which thou renderest.

Elizabeth Barrett Browning

Tell Him So

If you hear a kind word spoken
Of some worthy soul you know,
It may fill her heart with sunshine
If you only tell her so.

If a deed, however humble,
Helps you on your way to go,
Seek the one whose hand has helped you,
Seek him out and tell him so.

If your heart is touched and tender
Toward a sinner, lost and low,
It might help him to do better
If you'd only tell him so.

Oh my sisters, oh my brothers,
As o'er life's rough path you go,
If God's love has saved and kept you,
Do not fail to tell Him so.

Author Unknown

Monarch on Butterfly Weed
Gay Bumgarner

Joy of Life

Evening Breake
Redwoods National Park, Californ
H. Armstrong Rober

Every man's life is a fairy tale, written by God's fingers.

Hans Christian Andersen

Afternoon on a Hill

I will be the gladdest thing
  Under the sun!
I will touch a hundred flowers
  And not pick one.

I will look at cliffs and clouds
  With quiet eyes,
Watch the wind bow down the grass,
  And the grass rise.

And when lights begin to show
  Up from the town,
I will mark which must be mine,
  And then start down.

Edna St. Vincent Millay

Look to This Day

Look to this day!

For it is life,
The very life of life.
In its brief course
Lie all the verities
And realities of your existence:
The bliss of growth;
The glory of action;
The splendor of beauty;

For yesterday
Is already a dream,
And tomorrow
Is only a vision;
But today, well lived,
Makes every yesterday
A dream of happiness,
And every tomorrow
A vision of hope.

Look well, therefore, to this day!

from the Sanskrit

Mt. Hood, Cascade Mountains
Oregon
Ed Cooper

This Moment

I may never see tomorrow; there's no written guarantee,
And things that happened yesterday belong to history.
I cannot predict the future, and I cannot change the past.
I have just the present moment; I must treat it as my last.

I must use this moment wisely for it soon will pass away,
And be lost to me forever as a part of yesterday.
I must exercise compassion, help the fallen to their feet,
Be a friend unto the friendless, make an empty life complete.

I must make this moment precious for it will not come again,
And I can never be content with things that might have been.
Kind words I fail to say this day may ever be unsaid,
For I know not how short may be the path that lies ahead.

The unkind things I do today may never be undone,
And friendships that I fail to win may nevermore be won.
I may not have another chance on bended knee to pray,
And thank my God with humble heart for giving me this day.

I may never see tomorrow, but this moment is my own.
It's mine to use or cast aside; the choice is mine, alone.
I have just this precious moment in the sunlight of today,
Where the dawning of tomorrow meets the dusk of yesterday.

Paul F. Barnett

My Heart's in the Highlands

My heart's in the Highlands, my heart is not here;
My heart's in the Highlands a-chasing the deer;
A-chasing the wild deer, and following the roe,
My heart's in the Highlands, wherever I go.
Farewell to the Highlands, farewell to the North,
The birth place of Valour, the country of Worth,
Wherever I wander, wherever I rove,
The hills of the Highlands for ever I love.

Farewell to the mountains high cover'd with snow;
Farewell to the straths and green valleys below;
Farewell to the forests and wild hanging woods;
Farewell to the torrents and loud pouring floods.
My heart's in the Highlands, my heart is not here,
My heart's in the Highlands a-chasing the deer;
Chasing the wild deer, and following the roe;
My heart's in the Highlands, wherever I go.

Robert Burns

Be Strong

Be strong!
We are not here to play,
    to dream, to drift,
We have hard work to do
    and loads to lift.
Shun not the struggle,
    face it — 'tis God's gift.

Be strong!
Say not the days are evil.
    Who's to blame?
And fold the hands and acquiesce—
    O shame!
Stand up, speak out, and bravely,
    in God's name.

Be strong!
It matters not how deep
    entrenched the wrong,
How hard the battle goes,
    the day how long;
Faint not —fight on!
    Tomorrow comes the song.

Maltbie Davenport Babcock

Two Carefree Days

There are two days in the week about
    which and upon which I never worry.
Two carefree days, kept sacredly free
    from fear and apprehension.
One of these days is Yesterday.

Yesterday with all its cares and frets,
    with all its pains and aches, all its faults, and its
    mistakes and blunders, has passed forever beyond
    the reach of my recall.
I cannot undo an act that I wrought.
I cannot unsay a word that I said on Yesterday.

All that it holds of my life, of wrong, regret, and sorrow
    is in the hands of the Mighty Love that can bring honey
    out of the rock and sweet waters out of the bitterest desert.

And the other day I do not worry about is Tomorrow.
Tomorrow with all its possible adversities, its burdens,
    its perils, its large promise and poor performance,
    its failures and mistakes, is as far beyond the reach
    of my mastery as its dead sister, Yesterday.

Robert J. Burdette

The Wild Joys of Living

Oh, the wild joys of living!
The leaping from rock
Up to rock,
The strong rending of boughs
From the fir-tree,
The cool silver shock
Of the plunge
In a pool's living water,
The hunt of the bear,
And the sultriness
Showing the lion
Is couched in his lair.

Robert Browning

But they that wait upon the Lord
shall renew their strength;

They shall mount up
with wings as eagles,

They shall run, and not be weary;
and they shall walk, and not be faint.

Isaiah 40:31